DEM⊙S

Demos is an independent think-tank committed to radical thinking on the long-term problems facing the UK and other advanced industrial societies.

It aims to develop the ideas - both theoretical and practical - that will help to shape the politics of the 21st century, and to improve the breadth and quality of political debate.

Demos publishes books and a quarterly journal and undertakes substantial empirical and policy-oriented research projects. It also runs a permanent computer conference. **Demos** is a registered charity.

In all its work **Demos** brings together people from a wide range of backgrounds in business, academia, government, the voluntary sector and the media to share and cross-fertilise ideas and experiences.

For further information and subscription details please write to:

Demos
9 Bridewell Place
London EC4V 6AP

tel: 0171 353 4479
fax: 0171 353 4481
email: ...@demos.demon.co.uk

First published in 1995
by
Demos
9 Bridewell Place
London EC4V 6AP
tel: 0171 353 4479
fax: 0171 353 4481

Paper No. 12

ISBN 1 898309 16 7

Cover design by Adrian Taylor

Printed in Great Britain by
White Dove Press
London
Typesetting by Bartle & Wade Associates

The Creative City

Charles Landry
and
Franco Bianchini

Acknowledgements

This publication draws on ideas being developed in the context of the European Creative City Observatory initiated jointly by STADTart Dortmund: Ralph Ebert and Fritz Gnad with Klaus R. Kunzmann (University of Dortmund) and Comedia: Charles Landry and Franco Bianchini (De Montfort University, Leicester).

We are grateful to the Anglo-German Foundation for the Study of Industrial Society for funding the Creative City workshop held in Glasgow in May 1994 and Glasgow City Council and Glasgow Development Agency for their additional support.

We would like to thank the following for their help in researching and criticising this text: Geoff Mulgan, Ray Cunningham, Peter Hall, Ralph Ebert, Fritz Gnad, Liz Greenhalgh, Charles Handy, Klaus R. Kunzmann, Louise Rogers, Robert Rogerson, Lia Ghilardi Santacatterina, Aleks Sierz, Massimo Torrigiani, Ken Worpole and Perri 6, most of whom attended the workshop.

We would also like to thank the other participants in The Creative City workshop: Ken Bartlett, Keith Bassett, Jude Bloomfield, Ugo Businaro, Steve Charter, Jurgen Friedrichs, Rolf Funck, Chris Gentle, James Gibson, Michael Hayes, Steve Inch, Andrew Kelly, Kevin Kane, Jolanta Dziembowska-Kowalska, Heinrich Maeding, Martin zur Nedden, Heinz Schwarzbach, Peter Waterman, Klaus Wermker and David Wyles. The participants included representatives from five British and five German cities: Bristol, Cologne, Dresden, Essen, Glasgow, Karlsruhe, Kirklees, Leicester, Milton Keynes and Unna.

Contents

Preface

British city economies are in structural crisis, and the recession of the 1990s has exposed the fact that the crisis is even deeper than once supposed; it affects not only the manufacturing sector, long seen as a source of weakness but also whole swathes of the producer services. Hardly any part of the urban economy, any more, is completely free from the threat of overseas competition and offshoring. Business services and software, just as much as engineering, can be relocated in South India or the Pearl River Delta. This fact prompts the drastic question: What, if anything, could now provide the basis for urban economic revival?

One answer is to move into a wider range of services, until recently thought to be hardly part of the serious economy at all; culture, entertainment, sport, education. Up and down the land, cities are scrambling to develop this facet of their economies, once regarded as unserious and even effete. Another, even wider, answer is to argue that as cities seek to solve their own problems, they find answers that can be exported. The success of a city like Curitiba in Brazil, ultimate innovative city of the 1980s, provides a model.

The two prescriptions are of course not exclusive. Cities, regions and nations can prove innovative in more than one way; they can innovate culturally, technologically, or urbanistically. All three ways can potentially provide jobs and a source of invisible exports.

This is why *The Creative City* is immensely important. For it is one of the very first studies in the English language to reflect the existence of these diverse sources of innovation. Its case studies describe some of the most important policy initiatives worldwide today. Its general analysis is immensely provocative. At a time when existing theories are tired and exhausted, it provides a highly important intellectual way forward. It will surely prove to be one of the seminal studies of the 1990s.

Peter Hall
Bartlett School of Planning
University College London

Introduction

This short publication explores what it means to be a creative city. It sets out both why creativity has become more important to cities - why nurturing it is important for economic success -and how creativity can be mobilised to help solve the myriad problems of the city, with lateral, synthetic, cross-disciplinary approaches.

The first part explains what is new about the interlocking crises facing many cities. Secondly, we ask what creativity is and how it can be harnessed to make city life better. It argues that the hard sciences of urban planning need to be enriched by mobilising the experiences of different disciplines and people currently marginalised from decision making. In the last two chapters we show, by quoting examples from all over the world, how it is possible to be creative in practice, how obstacles to creativity can be overcome and how creative milieux can be established.

The Creative City is the result of a long period of research and consultancy on the problems and possibilities of cities in Europe. Over the last decade we have worked in more than 100 towns and cities ranging from Stirling to St. Petersburg, Middlesbrough to Milan, Huddersfield to Helsinki and Basingstoke to Barcelona. Much of this work was concerned with developing the artistic, cultural and social life of cities. But the lessons which were learnt seemed to have wider significance.

Meanwhile, Professor Klaus Kunzmann at the University of Dortmund and Ralph Ebert and Fritz Gnad at STADTart, also in Dortmund, were analysing urban and regional development, particularly in the Ruhr area, where a dramatic shift from traditional to more technologically advanced industry and services had taken place.

Our joint experience suggested that a new way of thinking was needed that went beyond traditional professional specialisations. In thinking through which lessons from the UK could benefit German cities and vice versa it seemed to us that the overriding feature common to the two countries was the importance of creative responses to urban problems, be they in traffic management, business development, greening the city, integrating ethnic communities, regenerating run down housing estates or enlivening city centres. Together we organised The Creative City workshop in Glasgow in May 1994 as a first step in what is intended to be a long-term project of research and practical initiatives which explore the creative potential of cities worldwide.

The Urban Crisis and the Role of Creativity in Cities

Why talk about creativity in relation to cities? In part the reason is obvious. Historically, creativity has always been the lifeblood of the city. Cities have always needed creativity to work as markets, trading and production centres, with their critical mass of entrepreneurs, artists, intellectuals, students, administrators and power-brokers. They have mostly been the places where races and cultures mix and where interaction creates new ideas, artefacts and institutions. And they have been the places which allow people room to live out their ideas, needs, aspirations, dreams, projects, conflicts, memories, anxieties, loves, passions, obsessions and fears.

But there are special reasons for thinking about the problems of cities today in terms of creativity - or the lack of it. Today many of the world's cities face tough periods of transition. Old industries are disappearing, as value-added is created less through what we manufacture and more through the application of new knowledge to products, processes and services. The factors that once shaped city development - transport, rivers, proximity of raw materials - have become less relevant. Distribution can now be managed from out of town centres. Transport is now a smaller proportion of overall production costs. Factories can be built on greenfield sites.

New sets of problems have risen up the agenda, partly as a result of the decay of the old shared rhythms of life and work, based on the factory and office: crime and insecurity; coping with globalisation and instant information; improving the quality of the everyday environment. At the very least, as in any time of transition, there is an acute need to go beyond inherited assumptions and ways of working.

But there is an additional reason why creativity is central to any thinking about the cities of the next century. Whereas the dominant industries of the 20th and 19th centuries depended on materials and industry, science and technology, the industries of the 21st century will depend increasingly on the generation of knowledge through creativity and innovation matched with rigorous systems of control. This is as true of the brokers engaged in trading derivatives as it is of television programme makers, software programmers and even theatrical impresarios. Achieving success in all these areas requires creative, interdisciplinary, holistic thinking - qualities that depend on subtle, supportive city milieux to promote them.

In the inter-urban competition game, being a base for knowledge-intensive firms and institutions, such as universities, research centres or the cultural industries, has acquired a new strategic importance. Future competition between nations, cities and enterprises looks set to be based less on natural resources, location or past reputation and more on the ability to develop attractive images and symbols and project these effectively. Indeed the urban renewal process can itself become a spectacle, as, in David Harvey's words, aesthetics comes to replace ethics in contemporary urban planning.[1]

It is hardly surprising then, that many of the older ways of thinking about cities have not kept up with the speed of change. But the task now is not simply to replace one set of simple paradigms with another. Instead we need to complement existing ways of thinking with new mindsets and additional methods for coping with change.

Cities, of course, have always been places of opportunity and problems, change and crisis. At many times the challenges they have thrown up - overcrowding, disease, social disorder, conflicts over land and its uses, a lack of infrastructure - have been tackled in creative and innovative ways. In the period after the Industrial Revolution the priority was to respond to immediate problems by creating physical infrastructures - sewage systems to contain disease and improve public health; housing to accommodate ever expanding populations; roads and railways to increase mobility for people and products. What was needed then was the particular creativity of engineers, planners and scientists.

In many ways their achievements were remarkable. As a comparative glance to the emerging mega-cities of the East, Africa and Latin America shows, Western cities have overcome many basic problems of urban living, with good public transport systems, control of most diseases and pollution.

In this century the main solutions went a step further, based on the theories of how to create 'the good city' associated with authors like Patrick Geddes[2], Lewis Mumford[3] or Jane Jacobs.[4] They emphasised not only how a city might be shaped physically but also what could improve the lived experience of cities for people. Yet when these ideas were taken up by the emerging planning profession, they were interpreted mainly in physical terms, disregarding the more subtle psychological effects on people. Often answers were arrived at by breaking problems into their component parts and providing a physical solution. The idea of zoning, to separate dirty industry from housing or commerce; grid-like street patterns to ease movement; or alternatively more fine-grained urban patterns to encourage interaction; height restrictions to protect skylines; the garden city movement to bring out the best of town and country. And this, even though the theorists realised that everything interconnects - the way a building is put together or a city laid out, affects how people feel about it and that in turn shapes their attitudes, motivations and behaviour.

But today the focus on the physical has gone as far as it can. For example, we know that a road or telecom network on its own will not create the kinds of innovative milieux that encourage people to interact and participate, but rather that this depends on the capacity to build partnerships by bringing institutions like universities together with local firms to develop new products. We know that crime will be solved less by physical control and more by establishing a sense of place and mutual responsibilities in communities and neighbourhoods.

We know that more sustainable environments will not be created if we only look at the environmental dimension; we also have to address how people mix and connect, their motivations and whether they take responsibility and 'own' where they live and change their lifestyles appropriately. To make cities respond to change we need to assess how 'feel', ambience, atmosphere and 'soft' infrastructures are created, something which requires different skills from those of planners brought up to think in terms of physical solutions.

Failure to do this has encouraged pessimism. As one writer put it:

"Our city of the future seems full of lights and shadows. Information workers may grow wealthy but the other ranks will be poor indeed. Video cameras may reassure but at the expense of building walls between different sectors of society. The car may help suburban shopping centres and edge cities to flourish but kill the old city centres and lead us up a blind alley where no form of public transport functions".[5]

This pessimism reflects the fear that a cluster of new problems has become visible.

One is division. The cities which are the nerve centres of the new global knowledge economy - London, New York, Frankfurt, Tokyo and Los Angeles - are increasingly socially fragmented, their labour markets divided between highly paid managers, technologists and professionals skilled in transnational law, government and business procedures, and employees - many of whom are women or from ethnic minorities - in less skilled, low paid, low status and often part-time service jobs.

Another is fear and alienation. Growth and prosperity have not ushered in an era of safety. Instead almost all cities have become more frightening to their inhabitants, albeit with the fear often out of proportion to the reality. Increasing mobility of criminals means that no area is safe from crime. Attempts are being made to shield areas and make them as safe as possible, sometimes by cutting them off or controlling them through closed circuit television (CCTV) systems. This is the case of many indoor shopping malls as well as corporate plazas, executive housing developments and even some affluent residential streets. In places like Bournemouth, Doncaster, Glasgow and Plymouth CCTV systems have reduced crime, but technology is becoming a substitute for people and the natural surveillance that comes from human interaction. Other local authorities, following the example of Wandsworth in London, are responding by creating their own security forces to compensate for the inadequacies of the police force.

A third common theme is dissatisfaction with the physical environment. As cars have become ever more dominant so have the tensions between the needs of drivers and those of others; conflicts that arise over such things as inner city ring roads, parking spaces, measures to control and slow traffic. At the same time there is concern about city centres and high streets. While high streets are dominated by the same names across the world, many town centres have been sucked dry of life by shopping centres out of town. There are many signs of a reaction against these trends - the search for authentic local products and experiences and 'heritage attractions' - but these seem to come too late.

Fourth, alongside anxiety about failing physical infrastructures, there is growing awareness that greater mobility for some combines with minimal mobility for others - the elderly, young parents - locked in by lack of transport and money, and by fear.

Fifth, there is the diminishing sense of locality, of shared place and identity that has made cities less clearly defined as places. Communities are now increasingly defined on the basis of common interests rather than in geographical terms. Even at the level of the neighbourhood there is often no community, because the factors that give rise to it - social homogeneity, immobility and the need to co-operate[6] - are no longer there. One sign is the increasing number of neighbourhood disputes, which have led to the establishment of mediation services by many local authorities. The problem is compounded by unresolved issues around the settlement of former waves of immigrants, and by deliberate policies developed by the civil service and private companies to make sure that employees do not 'go native'. Bank, building society, insurance and retailing managers, as well as civil servants, tend to move every few years for career reasons. Those who remain have less access to power and resources to improve the quality of life of their communities.

Some of these senses of unease are not in themselves new. Nor is the continuing contrast between the glossy images of city development offered by architects, politicians, and others, and these feelings of despair and depression.

Descriptions of cities have always oscillated between inspiration and disillusionment. For many, and especially avant-garde artists, the city has meant excitement and liberation. Movements like Constructivism, Cubism and Futurism drew on urban sensibilities. Writers like Charles Baudelaire saw the city as a celebration of the artificial, the transient, the vibrant, but also the melancholy. At different times, the city has symbolised faith, as in the Heavenly City of New Jerusalem, or it has represented the heroism of modern life. It has stood for the discovery of the new, however ephemeral, fragmented or dislocated. On the dark side, the city has been viewed as a place of squalor, degradation and anomie. Descriptions of London in the novels of authors such as Charles Dickens or social surveys such as Henry Mayhew's *London Labour and the London Poor*, and Charles Booth's *Life and Labour of the People of London* paint a picture of social inequality and injustice. Equally German intellectuals such as Max Weber, Georg Simmel and Oswald Spengler were concerned with the cultural consequences of urban life. To them the expanding market economy and emerging large scale bureaucracies were key determinants of the urban experience, for they bred among city dwellers a character that was rational, impersonal, alienated, unemotional and autonomous.[7]

If anything this ambiguity has become more complex in the closing years of the century. Recent descriptions of the city as a decentred urban field suggest that it is increasingly difficult even to determine what a city is and what its contours are. Sprawling conurbations with diffuse centres and satellite estates lack boundaries and character, and become, in Melvin Webber's definition, the 'non-place urban realm'.[8]

Some conclude that the problems have become insoluble. We take a different view; that there is nothing insoluble or inevitable about new problems if we can put them in the proper focus and apply the right tools.

What is Creativity?

- *Creativity as an alternative to instrumental thinking*

The dominant intellectual traditions which have shaped urban policies have been profoundly rooted in a belief in the virtues of instrumental, rational and analytic thinking. In respect of planning, sewage, water, utilities, roads, these approaches helped to transform chaotic, disease-ridden cities into safe and healthy environments. But reasoning grounded in science, governed by logic, has its limits too. It compartmentalises knowledge into separate branches or boxes, imposing order over nature, without letting 'messy reality' get too much in the way. Worse, it makes it hard to cope with periods of change.

What we describe as creative thinking is a way of getting rid of rigid preconceptions and of opening ourselves to complex phenomena which cannot always be dealt with in a strictly logical manner. It is also a way of discovering previously unseen possibilities. Everybody is potentially creative, but organisational structures, habits of mind and working practices can squeeze creativity out. Logical/rational/technical reasoning is a useful tool, but it is only one of many. Just as a carpenter can't build a table with only a hammer, so we need a richer and more refined mental tool kit to identify and address today's problems.

How can we define creativity? There is an extensive literature on creativity, drawing from psychology and aesthetics. Some have offered precise definitions and measurements for individuals taking tests, although one of the flaws of this literature is that high scores do not prove that one will be creative in one's own vocation. Creativity has been analysed in relation to motivation and personality, to upbringing and formative experience. In the work of Mihaly Czikszentmihalyi it has been linked to the experience of flow, intense moments of absorption. And in the work of the American psychologist Howard Gardner it has been linked to leadership.

Much of the literature draws on the etymological roots of the word, seeing creativity as about bringing something into existence, generating, inventing, dealing imaginatively with seemingly intractable problems. The connotations of the verb to create are positive; nearly all of its opposites are negative, including to destroy, to kill and to abolish. (Of course, creativity can be an overused concept; for example, any literary work, whatever its merits, can be called creative writing.)[9]

But most agree that genuine creativity involves thinking a problem afresh and from first principles; experimentation; originality; the capacity to rewrite rules; to be unconventional; to discover common threads amid the seemingly disparate; to look at situations laterally and with flexibility. These ways of thinking encourage innovation and generate new possibilities. In this sense, creativity is a 'modernist' concept because it emphasises the new, progress and continual change.

- Synthetic Creativity

Every period in history seems to need its own forms of creativity. Dealing with the impacts of the industrial era required society to harness the creativity of engineers and scientists who broke down problems into their component parts. Today, in our judgement, we need a completely different type of creativity, as increasingly we know more facts but understand less. In particular, we need the creativity of being able to synthesize, to connect, to gauge impacts across different spheres of life, to see holistically, to understand how material changes affect our perceptions, to grasp the subtle ecologies of our systems of life and how to make them sustainable. We need, in other words, the skills of the broker, the person who can think across disciplines, the networker, the connector - a 'softer' set of skills.

- *Ridding ourselves of preconceptions about creativity*

Before explaining the practical consequences of this type of creativity some preconceptions need clearing up. One is that creativity is a natural talent that cannot be learned. Edward de Bono eloquently points out that while natural creativity exists in some people, it can also be taught. How this might be done is elaborated in his book *Serious Creativity*.

A further preconception is that creative people are always rebels. Conformists, it is assumed, are attached to existing ways of doing something, whereas rebels challenge rules and strike out. As de Bono notes, their momentum is generated by being *against* something. However, as the techniques of creative thinking can be taught and encouraged it may well be that the creativity of conformists is more constructive, perhaps because it is better focused. Indeed Japan has produced many creative people although it is known as a very conformist society.

Linked to the idea of being rebellious is the idea that you have be crazy to be creative. As creativity can be about unconventional thinking, it is often assumed that the more inhibitions are lost and the more 'crazy' we become, the more creative we are being. Release from constraints may be necessary, but it is certainly not a sufficient condition for the development of creative ideas. Creativity for creativity's sake is not the answer. Certain brainstorming techniques reinforce this idea of craziness. But being creative is more than a hit and miss affair. Creativity is both about allowing a free flow of ideas and linking these new ideas to restraints, grammars and rules, and of course to reality.

Another distinction that needs to be made is between intelligence and creativity. Intelligence is the ability to perceive and comprehend meaning and is directly linked to the notion of intellect. As de Bono notes, intelligent people may initially be wary of putting forward seemingly frivolous and speculative ideas, because their critical/analytical faculties are so strong that they constantly question the words and concepts they use. Intelligence, in de Bono's words, is 'the potential of the mind... This is equivalent to the horsepower of a car'.[10] Creativity, however, is about changing the concepts and perceptions themselves. If allied to the analytical powers of intelligence, it can produce a very effective combination.

- Creativity and Innovation

The terms creativity and innovation are often used interchangeably, but they are distinct. According to Andy Burnett of the Centre for Creativity at the Cranfield School of Management: 'Creativity is a divergent thought process that generates ideas, and is non-evaluative; whereas innovation is a convergent process concerned with the selection and implementation of ideas'.[11] Creativity, in other words, is the process through which new ideas are produced, while innovation is the process through which they are implemented. A city may be very creative, but may not have the analytical, evaluative and financial skills to develop innovative solutions. Creativity is a necessary precondition for innovation, but innovation is what counts in maximising the potential of a city. Getting from creativity to innovation involves evaluation, which is not in itself part of the creative process. Evaluation involves assessing how appropriate an idea is to a given situation, its feasibility, cost-effectiveness and popularity. Some cities may specialise in creativity and others in innovation.

- *Creativity is context driven*

Creativity expresses itself differently in each areas of human activity. The Italian sociologist and clinical psychologist Alberto Melucci identifies six arenas: The arts, science, advertising and communication, organisation and business management, youth sub-cultures and collective movements.[12] At the moment most city governments have been inspired only by the two types of creativity which are easiest to understand and manage through instrumental rationality: Those of business organisations and of the advertising and communications world – for example, through the ever increasing number of city marketing campaigns being implemented.

Creativity needs to be communicated to the outside world in order to have an impact, otherwise it is purely self-expression. Melucci underlines the importance of an 'optimum threshold of resistance' in the relationship between the creative subject and the external environment.[13] In order to be creatively productive, an element of tension and hostility is required as a spur to further exploration and action, and to encourage receptiveness to ideas.

The appropriate threshold stands at a fine balance – if it is too intense it may overwhelm you, yet if it is absent it may not initiate a sufficient response. The degree to which a creative act throws light on a problem depends on appropriate timing, both for the creator and the recipient. There are ideas whose purchase is limited by the fact that they are ahead of their time. Some ideas need to mature much longer than processes of creative thinking in many enterprises and city administrations are prepared to allow. Creativity is not solely about the new – it also involves opening ourselves out to ideas, influences and resources that are all around us, that we cannot control totally, yet that can be harnessed to making our lives richer and more sustainable.

- *The consequences of instrumental rationality*

What are the implications of the dominance of instrumental rationality for urban planning? Both geography and planning –the disciplines concerned with the description, management and transformation of places – are dominated by the analysis and manipulation of data expressed in a quantifiable form, so that 'scientific' decisions can be arrived at. This approach has tended to leave out other descriptions of reality, which are subjective and not quantifiable: memory, emotions, passions, senses, desires, all of which engender motivations and loyalties. It is likely that a more humanistic and culturally aware approach would have prevented the destruction of many English town and city centres by insensitive planning in the 1950s and 1960s. Mark Girouard, in his book *The English Town*, comments:

"I went back to Huddersfield and found that its heroic streets of mills had long since vanished under a ring road... I saw how ruthlessly two-thirds of the centre of Worcester and most of the centre of Gloucester had been mangled; walked from the station to the shire hall through the corpse of what had once been Chelmsford; discovered how Taunton had destroyed in a year or two the town centre so carefully and creatively formed in the 18th century; wandered in Liverpool past gutted buildings and over the acres of desert, which had once been covered by 18th century squares and terraces; and wept in the screaming desolation of central Birmingham... Keeping and understanding the past makes for tolerance; it also makes for creativity, in devising ways of altering and adding to towns, for nothing comes out of a vacuum. It is hard to believe that those who made the running in English towns in the 1950s and 1960s would have done what they did if they had known more about them."[14]

While the ravages of the 1950s and 1960s have fortunately abated, there is still not sufficient understanding of how a sense of place can be created, maintained or recreated. The debate about urban sustainability highlights the links between the natural, physical, social, cultural, political and economic environments and is thus encouraging holistic thinking. Yet our institutions for decision-making about cities are still largely based on rigid functional specialisations, without sufficient sharing and co-operation between different departments, disciplines and sectors.

The implication is that we need to enrich the 'scientific' and quantitativist tradition with insights gained from more qualitative, human-oriented approaches – ranging from history and philosophy to religion and the arts. Planners find it easier to think in terms of expenditure on highways, car parks and physical redevelopment schemes rather than on soft infrastructures such as training initiatives for skills enhancement, the encouragement of a lively night-time economy, grants to voluntary organisations to develop social networks or social innovations and the decentralisation of powers to build up local capacity and encourage people to have a stake in the running of their neighbourhoods.

One symptom of the narrowness of planners' horizons is the fact that they find it very hard to focus on desires rather than needs. According to our definition, a need is an objectifiable entity: 'I need a lamp post outside my front door'; 'I need a more frequent bus service'; 'I need more policemen on the beat in the town centre'. A desire, by contrast, involves your subconscious, a personal engagement, dreams and feelings, and the atmosphere and feeling of a place.

- Thinking more holistically

There are different and seemingly contradictory types of creativity. For example, there is the creativity of aggressive intervention and the creativity of holding back; the creativity

16

of innocence and child-like naivety and the creativity of experience. Innocence is the ability to be surprised, curious, fresh and unencumbered by previous knowledge, but it entails the danger of ignorance. Experience, on the contrary, involves accumulated knowledge about similar situations, but it can be constraining.

The challenge of creativity is to recognise that opposites can be parts of the same whole. Here are some examples:

- Any intervention in the urban fabric – such as building a new road – inevitably touches citizens' lives and elicits responses from them. The greening of urban motorways in the Ruhr and Stuttgart – with extensive noise shields made from luxuriant shrubs and trees, producing a wooded linear park landscape – is an example of simultaneously dealing with accessibility, noise, aesthetics and ecology. The planners had to think laterally to come up with this idea.

- Our deepest feelings about the city are at the moment expressed only on special occasions, such as carnivals and festivals, which are clearly separated from 'normal' activities. The creative energies which are generated on some of these occasions are rarely carried over into the mainstream of city life. By contrast, for example, the Palio in Siena – a twice-yearly horse race taking place in the historic Piazza del Campo – involves citizens from all neighbourhoods and is a powerful symbol motivating and unifying the city. It gives the people of Siena the courage and confidence to channel their creativity into maintaining a way of life and an urban fabric which elsewhere have been destroyed.

- City planners and politicians have often been accused of favouring 'masculine' solutions such as large-scale redevelopment or inter-urban competition. A more 'feminine' approach might have different priorities, such as a focus on soft infrastructure, ambience or collaboration between cities. Helsinki, for example, has been less ravaged by large-scale redevelopment of its historic centre than many other European capitals. It has paid greater attention to comfort, the needs of women, minorities and ecology. Helsinki's 'soft' approach to urban creativity is evident in many fields: in the very high standards of insulation and heating in public buildings and transport; the availability of creches; the excellent facilities for disabled people; a harmonisation of new housing with the natural environment; the levels of cultural provision for the Swedish minority; the openness to initiatives by international organisations and the pleasantly slow rhythm of city life.

- The shape of cities and their strategies for future development are largely planning-led with an emphasis on order and coherence. Yet the vitality of cities is often determined by unplanned, slightly chaotic development. Spontaneity may need to be encouraged just as much as control or management – there are right times for anarchy and right times for rules, right times for self-expression and right times for control. Good examples of the appropriate balance between anarchy and rules are street markets such as Camden Lock and Portobello Road in London, where within a controlled framework unplanned, unlicensed and coincidental activities can take place, including street performances and occasional stalls.

•   The initiatives and intuitions of citizens can be just as valid as the rationality of planners, policy-makers and public administrators. Examples include: the development of local currencies based on the exchange of services within Local Exchange and Trading Systems (LETS), which the Inland Revenue finds difficult to cope with because no money changes hands; initiatives by local residents to block off roads used by joyriders, in response to the inertia of the local authority; the alternative proposals for the development of a large area behind King's Cross station by local community groups; the occupation by young people of redundant buildings in many Italian cities, to create a network of social centres which attempt to address failures in provision for youth.

These examples confirm that although desires are multifarious and different for each individual, they can be grouped into manageable practical programmes for action corresponding to different communities of interest.

How to Become a Creative City

- *Removing obstacles to creativity*

Accountability, bureaucracy and crisis management - Before you can build a creative environment you need to remove obstacles. These come in many shapes and forms.

Cities are largely run by public officials who must be accountable to electorates. This slows down the pace of response to problems, which tends to be faster in private enterprises. On the other hand, more open accountability could turn this potential liability into an asset by creating channels for a flow of creative ideas from the citizens to city governments, just as the best companies tap their workforce and customers for good ideas. In practice this rarely happens because politicians and officers are afraid both of raising public expectations which cannot be met, and perhaps of threatening their own legitimacy.

The second reason why bureaucracies block creativity is their responsibility for keeping the urban machine running. This usually involves complex rules and regulations such as planning permissions, licences, bye-laws and traffic restrictions. Rules of this kind tend to be long-lasting, and for good reasons, resistant to change. But bureaucratic mindsets frequently imbue the whole organisation.

Thirdly, there is the view that 'if it ain't broke don't fix it'. Like many other pieces of conventional wisdom this has some truth in it. But it can be harmful. It means that issues are only addressed when they become problems. Responses, as a consequence, are defined by the problems themselves, or in the context of crisis, and do not explore other alternatives.[15]

Shortsightedness - The short-term logic of professional politicians, and non-elected agencies – which aim chiefly at obtaining quick and visible results – prevents them laying the foundations for longer-term solutions. One example is the work of the London Docklands Development Corporation, which neglected the need for long-term infrastructure and social planning in areas such as transport and training, with very damaging consequences for the success of its regeneration strategy. Another is the tendency among many local authorities to invest heavily in flagship buildings and events. The relative failure of the 1991 World Student Games in Sheffield, and current debates in Birmingham about the impact of heavy investment in the International Convention Centre are cases in point.

Patronage - Networks of patronage and long-established elites reduce freedom of access to power and information. This has become as true of the networks of quangos that run much of the UK public sector as it has long been of areas ruled by one party. In each case, ossified elites lose the means to draw on the creativity of the people they are meant to serve.

The power of the professions - The training base for the professions is frequently too narrow to make creative connections. This is as true for town planners, steeped in the disciplines of land use and development control, as it is for engineers, librarians, leisure managers and environmental health officers. Professionals develop their own technical jargon, which obscures communication with the outside world difficult and constrains their own thinking. They also have systems for legitimising their actions, often based on evidence which fails to stand up to scrutiny from a wider perspective. For instance, traffic engineers stress the need for blank visual environments so as not to distract motorists, without considering the impact of such degraded environments on residents and visitors.

- Laying the foundations for a creative milieu

What are the pre-conditions for establishing a creative city, and what can policy makers do about it? We would highlight twelve key themes:

Reassessing success and failure - In most organisations, especially public sector ones, risk is frowned on and failure not sanctioned. Politicians and bureaucrats, in particular, are reluctant to admit failure. Unlike business, they have no internal research and development mechanism to weed out failure and analyse appropriate risks. Yet failure may contain the seeds of future success – if it is analysed and not automatically punished. Reflecting on failure is beneficial as it becomes a learning device. It should be possible to distinguish between 'competent' and 'incompetent' failure. Success, on the other hand, often leads to complacency. Being creative does not mean you will necessarily be successful. Each creative project is a pilot from which we can learn something. Many people who have subsequently become successful have failed in the past.

New indicators of success - There is a vast risk assessment literature for investment decisions, but the equivalent for more socially oriented projects remains undeveloped. This means that indicators of cost-effectiveness that go beyond traditional cost-benefit analysis need to be developed. Many are now involved in devising such indicators. The New Economics Foundation has been one important source. Their indicators have suggested that the quality of life in Britain may have declined over the last 20 years even while GDP has nearly doubled. Cities have been particularly subject to rising indirect costs (such as congestion or declining air quality) which are not picked up by traditional measures. With the help of NEF a group of UK cities is now developing a new set of quality indicators to better evaluate policy successes and failures.

Handling capacity - To handle creative ideas well, and turn them into workable projects, cities need what could be termed handling capacity. This is not just a matter of adminitrative competence. It is also about encouraging people to think holistically. Clearcut professional responsibilities are necessary for efficiency and responsibility, but they need to be supplemented by much more team working and partnerships, helped by brokers and social entrepreneurs, if creativity is to become a normal part of city governance.

Making the most of creative individuals - Creative projects are generally driven by committed – sometimes obsessed or eccentric – individuals. Their 'creative deviance' needs to be positively sanctioned. In local authorities this might mean that grants for innovation and pilot projects are made available, deliberately shaped to encourage experiment. For the same reasons it may often be important to introduce outside attitudes and skills, to encourage a more critical, imaginative view of how things are done.

The contribution of immigrants - Settled immigrants are outsiders and insiders at the same time. Because of their backgrounds they have different ways of looking at problems and different priorities. This can give a creative impulse to a city. Peter Burke has studied the way in which groups such as the Jewish community have historically helped cities – such as Vienna, Amsterdam or Antwerp – to re-invigorate themselves.[16] Asian immigrants in Britain have been instrumental in saving the neighbourhood corner shop and have taken the lead in extending trading hours, revitalising parts of cities at night and at weekends. Equally the Italian, Chinese and Asian immigrants have enriched our food culture as well as bringing new ways of doing business. The key point is the need for a balance between maintaining a separate identity and integrating into the majority community.

Using catalysts - Catalyst events and organisations can create opportunities for people with different perspectives to come together and share ideas. A US-inspired organisation, Common Purpose, has a year-long programme in a number of European cities, bringing together operational managers from diverse sectors, such as health, education, the arts, the media, local government, business and charities. The objective is to create mutual understanding of the city's problems and possibilities and in this way, to develop a leadership group able to address issues comprehensively. Urban Design Action Teams (UDAT) and Planning for Real procedures encourage people with different backgrounds and skills to focus on a particular problem, often with brilliant and unexpected results. Public spaces can also act as catalysts by attracting different types of people and encouraging interaction. Synergy is also achieved in managed workspaces where people can support each other and exchange ideas.

Balancing cosmopolitanism and locality - Good ideas can be garnered from national and international competitions, which are currently limited to architectural and urban design projects. Competitions and exhibitions could also be used for social experiments, such as dealing with drugs and crime, and for environmental and economic development purposes. Internationally oriented policies are valuable because competition and benchmarking comparison with other cities provides stimulus. The brokering of new economic, scientific and cultural collaborations is a key to the future prosperity of cities. The organisation of and participation in trade fairs, the membership of international networks of cities, cultural and educational exchanges, twinning, staff exchanges, co-operation between research centres, are some of the things that can be done to enhance the receptiveness, open-mindedness and international orientation of a city. But cities must strike a balance between cosmopolitanism and local roots. If local identity is eroded too much, a city may lose confidence and sense of direction. International initiatives should co-exist with festivals and other celebrations and rituals designed to strengthen local identity.[17]

From multiculturalism to interculturalism - External influences can be re-elaborated creatively through local culture and hybrid identities can emerge, such as Glaswegian Chinese or Afro-Caribbean Scouser. These cultural hybrids matter because creativity arises more from interculturalism than multiculturalism. Many social and cultural policies have aimed at multiculturalism, which means the strengthening of the separate cultural identities of ethnic minorities, which now have their own arts centres, schools, places of worship and social clubs. But multiculturalism can be problematic if there is little communication between cultures. We now need to move one stage further. Resources should be directed more to intercultural projects which build bridges between the fragments, and produce something new out of the multicultural patchwork of our cities. Creativity may be encouraged by fragmentation, but not by marginalisation. Ethnic ghettoes are unlikely to contribute to solving the wider problems of cities. Ignorance and suspicion are among the root causes of racism and greater intercultural understanding can help foster social cohesion. New ideas can be generated through cultural crossovers, as in the success of young British Asians who have synthsised 'bhangra' music.

Participation is more than a slogan - Participation can be encouraged through means such as citizen audits and juries where a representative selection of local citizens assesses the performance of local authorities and other public sector organisations. Participation creates ownership; people are more likely to become stakeholders in projects they have participated in. For example, if people are involved in the design and management of their housing estates, this can help in fostering a culture that reduces crime and vandalism.

Developing creative spaces - Creative people and projects need to be based somewhere. A creative city requires land and buildings at affordable prices, preferably close to other cultural amenities. These are likely to be available in urban fringes and in areas where uses are changing, such as former port and industrial zones. Cheap spaces reduce financial risk and therefore encourage experiment. This has begun to happen in some old industrial areas close to city centres – for instance, the Duke Street area in Liverpool, Bradford's Little Germany and the Cultural Industries Quarter in Sheffield.

Early winners and staging posts - Momentum depends on starting with easier projects which become 'early winners'. A series of intermediate goals or staging posts have to be set, to make visible how the city is moving and to generate confidence and enthusiasm. This momentum in turn creates its own dynamics. Symbols can be used to facilitate this process. A prestigious new building can be the spur; as can an event like a festival or a conference; or new regulations such as relaxed licensing laws; or a mechanism like a new subsidy scheme; or the intervention of a committed individual or organisation; or, lastly, effective city marketing as in Glasgow and Montpellier.

Rethinking urban management - Across the world there has been a good deal of thinking about how city management needs to change to concentrate on the things it does best and contract out where it is weaker. Enabling authorities try not to be burdened by inappropriate tasks which are delegated to private, voluntary or semi-public organisations. At the same time they put more energy and resources into strategic oversight, anticipating citizens' demands and, crucially, investing in development and innovation.

In order to delegate, city stakeholders need vision and leadership. As the recent report *Quality of Life in Cities* by

Ken Young concludes: 'Experience from both Britain, Europe and America suggests that strong leadership is an essential element in both the social and economic regeneration of cities; conversely weak leadership is a significant contributor to urban decline.' He also stresses the importance of faith:

"Sometimes faith is a necessary precursor to investment, both in the sense of financial resources and of investing in a vision of the city... this requires an active leadership to promote and bolster an image of the city, which initially may bear only a limited resemblance to reality to the majority of citizens."[18]

Leadership in this context is not just about personalities, but rather about bringing together leaders from local politics, business and the voluntary sector to contribute to the development of the city.

Who is Being Creative and Where?

We have painted a somewhat bleak picture of the way cities are run. Many creative people working in administrations, businesses and voluntary organisations have tried and failed to change their cities. However, there are also many instances of interesting and innovative solutions to urban problems. In this chapter we highlight a few which indicate what can be done. One of the common features of these initiatives is the way they achieve results through perceptive, bold, farsighted, unlikely, shrewd or inspired combinations of ingredients. In other words their most obvious common theme is the application of a synthesising creativity, which brings together unexpected elements. What follows is a collection of vignettes, which we hope will provide inspiration.

- Reshaping the city

Urban design is essentially about knitting together different parts of the city into a coherent artefact. Some cities have been both courageous and sensitive in attempting to create – or recreate –an urban fabric which has been torn apart by roads and industries. In preparation for the 1992 Olympics, **Barcelona**'s city council created an imaginative network of over 150 interlinked public spaces, often etched out of the interstices between existing buildings and roads. They comprise pocket parks and squares often punctuated by fountains, mosaics and sculptures. They lighten up the townscape, reduce the claustrophobia of the densely packed city and provide much needed breathing space and recreation areas. They make people feel more relaxed, more motivated and more loyal to their city.

In **Melbourne**, after the first phase of rapid development of the central business district in the 1970s, the city's urban design team was able to push through a set of planning regulations that maintained the streetline at its Victorian height of four to eight storeys and concentrated the upward expansion of buildings within courtyards behind the blocks. As a consequence, when Melbourne is viewed from a distance it appears like a metropolis with a Manhattan skyline, but when seen from the street in the central district; it appears more human in scale. The street pattern has been retained and wind tunnels so often created by skyscrapers have been avoided. The result makes the city feel more friendly. This was a simple, yet bold, idea which involved keeping things as they were.

Another characteristic of Melbourne's skyline was produced by a local bye-law. This ruled that the view to the Anzac Memorial – Australia's monument to those who died in two world wars –should remain clear from a number of directions, including from the city's major thoroughfare, Swanston Street. As a consequence the shapes of many of the skyscrapers curve back to allow unimpeded sightlines. This means that, in contrast to the monolithic square blocks so prevalent elsewhere, the tops of Melbourne's buildings often boast interesting shapes. Thus, almost by accident, a restraining bye-law created positive side effects.

For years **Valencia** has had problems with the flooding of the river Turia, which winds its way for 12 kilometres through the city. To avoid flood damage, it was diverted around the city, and the former river bed turned into a linear urban park with children's playgrounds, cultural facilities, sports tracks, swimming pools, restaurants, cafés, cycleways and nature conservation areas. This bold move gave the city much needed green space, and created a quiet zone, as well as green links between parts of the city previously separated by the river.

Similar linear urban parks could be created in British cities by putting underground or digging up sections of inner ring roads.

These parks could include sports and leisure facilities, lakes, nature reserves, restaurants, cafés, schools, shops and housing, and allow the city centre to expand more organically and, in some cases, reunite itself. In Leicester, for example, an important historic and archaeological area is torn apart by the inner ring road, with the Guildhall on the inner edge, the Castle and the historic church of St Mary de Castro on the outer and the Magazine Gateway Museum stranded on a traffic island.

Policy-makers in **Cologne** responded to the fracturing that an urban throughway created in the city centre along the Rhine by putting it underground. This simple solution – which has been discussed in a number of other cities, including London – was undoubtedly costly, but it amply repaid the investment. The link between the centre and the rest of the city was re-established by creating a number of interconnected pedestrian public spaces. At their edges, entertainment facilities of all sorts have developed. The project resulted in increased use of nearby museums, helped develop a riverfront restaurant culture, enhanced the city centre and counteracted the trend towards out-of-town shopping. So successful has this intervention been that **Düsseldorf**, a few kilometres upstream, is now following suit.

An example of creative urban development going against the grain of narrowly commercial logic is that of **Rotterdam** in the second half of the 1970s. A new generation of Social Democratic politicians, who took office in 1974, were critical of the functionalist planning model based on a rational grid, which had informed the reconstruction of the city after the Second World War and whose symbol was the Lijnbaan central shopping area. The city centre was replanned according to an 'urban intensity model', mixing housing, recreation, promenading and cultural uses. In order to create an alternative to suburban lifestyles, liveliness and popular participation in city life became the new imperatives. Radical architects like Piet Blom were commissioned to build on prominent sites and encouraged to experiment. The resulting buildings are intricate, multifaceted and expressive in a deliberate reaction against the typical right angles of the orthogonal Lijnbaan. They are now popular landmarks in an area which could easily have become yet another office district built in the international corporate style.

- Urban cosmetics and theatrical illusions

Seemingly superficial, 'cosmetic' interventions can have an important effect on morale – and on how the city is seen by both residents and visitors. They prefigure what a place might become and make it easier to generate resources for future development. Often they prove so popular they become permanent. In **Genoa,** for example, striking *trompe d'oeil* panels were painted on a series of prominent harbour buildings next to dilapidated, pollution-encrusted blocks of flats and offices. Combined with architect Renzo Piano's new aquarium and belvedere tower, the panels project images of a better future for the area.

Though apparently incongruous, the refurbishment in pink colours of the shopping centre at **Elephant and Castle** in south London has, by simply using a coat of paint, transformed the image of a notoriously drab and profoundly unloved landmark. Turnover increased by over 10 per cent in the first year after refurbishment.

Within two weeks, the same developer created **Gabriel's Wharf** in an infill site between Waterloo and Blackfriars on the south bank of the Thames. This cheap and cheerful new market – with shops, restaurants and cafés – is housed in prefabricated and temporary buildings used by visitors, office workers and the residents of nearby Coin Street.

These examples show that creative solutions do not have to be expensive and permanent in order to be effective. Some politicians wrongly think that in order to leave a mark it is necessary to build monuments for posterity rather than to create environments people enjoy using.

One of the ugliest features of contemporary cities is the car park, usually either a drab expanse of soulless tarmac or a claustrophobic, multi-storey cement tomb. Places to be avoided, they are filled with cars in the day time and often dangerously empty at night. Yet some cities have been successful in humanising these unloved areas. For example, **Stuttgart** disguised the entrances to its underground car parks with vegetation, creating the playful impression of a natural cave. **Nice** used one of its prime central sites as a car park, but created the illusion of a Babylon-style hanging garden, which makes the car park appear like a piece of environmental art. The city of **Southampton** – ironically benefiting from planning gain resources from an ugly Toys'R'Us concession – created an ocean liner-shaped multi-storey car park, which is a positive addition to the urban landscape, and – with its numerous round windows – has a feeling of lightness.

Rational planners often find it hard to accept that the city is a stage on which the craft of urban design must be practised. This requires making connections with the city's history, architectural styles and popular preferences.

- The marriage of old and new

In **Paris**, I. M. Pei's glass pyramid in front of the Louvre is one of the city's new landmarks and has redefined that monumental complex and its relationship to the rest of the capital. Although it acts merely as a foyer, it is also an experience in itself. It gives access to an underground 'city within the city' – with shops, metro entrances, and public spaces – using the metaphor of the pyramid wherever possible. It is an extremely successful coupling of good quality, high-tech contemporary architecture with historical buildings.

In **Nîmes**, a city of about 100,000 inhabitants in southern France, Norman Foster and other prestigious architects have been commissioned by the council to insert high-tech structures in archaeological sites. Next to the Roman Maison Carrée Foster has built an uncompromisingly modernist mediatheque in glass. An ingenious roof was devised to cover the Roman arena, making it possible to use it throughout the year. Nîmes has used these projects symbolically to project an image of their city that, without forgetting its ancient roots, looks to the future with confidence.

Perugia, a city of similar size in central Italy, installed escalators, leading up several hundred metres to the cathedral square, in the steep rocky hill on which the city is built. These move past a series of open caves with permanent and temporary exhibitions, where light refracts in surprising ways from one level to the next. The construction helps free the narrow, medieval streets of the upper town from cars. An obvious and simple idea perhaps, but since initiatives like it are rare, it appears uncommonly courageous.

In north-western Italy, **Verona** uses its Roman arena in a variety of ways. Most well known is the summer opera festival. In the Christmas season, however, the location boasts an illuminated steel shooting star, which rests with its 20 white spikes in the square next to the amphitheatre. Its tail forms an 80-metre arch linking the square with the inside of the arena, where a successful international crib festival takes place. The idea emerged from an architectural competition sponsored by the Chamber of Commerce and acts like a magnet, attracting Christmas shoppers and visitors from all over Italy.

Since the early 1980s **Frankfurt** has invested in a Museums Quarter on the left bank of the Main. Of note here is the German Museum of Architecture, designed by O. M. Ungers, which has created an independent modern structure within the skin of an old building. Similarly, the Museum of Applied Arts is an old building linked through a glass tunnel to a larger, modern part built by Richard Meier.

In Britain there are very few examples where the old and the new are combined in such ways. Here it is more common to convert historic buildings without fundamentally altering their external appearance or to construct new buildings in mock historic styles. There are exceptions, however, such as the new public library in **Croydon** which is connected with the 19th century civic museum and constructed as an 'intelligent' 21st century building.

- Travelling hopefully

All successful transport systems are rooted in good design, yet the experience of travel is usually associated with boredom, irritation, and squalor. A number of cities have used artists in the development of transport schemes not as a marginal add-on, but as an integrated aspect of transport planning. **Stockholm**, **St Petersburg**, **Moscow** and **Boston** provide examples where this approach has been applied. In the two Russian cities each metro station is different and made distinctive by the work of engineers, architects, artists and artisans, using mosaics, frescoes, sculptures and domes. Stockholm is perhaps the best example of art contributing to public transport policy. The underground system comprises 101 stations, many of which have been decorated as part of a programme which began in the 1970s. Now more than half the stations are complete.

The best of these are major works of artistic imagination, architectural vigour and quality design. They bear comparison with the best of 20th century civic, religious and commercial architecture. Described as the 'world's largest art gallery', the Stockholm metro is not only a beautiful means of transport but also an attraction which draws visitors.[19]

In the Ruhr, a simple but effective bye-law – which provides car parking bays for women – has had a big impact on the social life of women by encouraging them to go out more at night. In **Dortmund**, a sign indicates that the area nearest the exit of a multi-storey car park is reserved for women. The cost of the sign and accompanying CCTV system is very small.

- *Walkability*

What is creative about most successful pedestrianisation schemes is that they are radical and broad-ranging solutions, often implemented in the teeth of fierce but shortsighted opposition. A decade ago, for example, **Groningen**, in the Netherlands, decided to become a walkable and cyclable city. The shopkeepers were initially against pedestrianisation, but are now clamouring for an extension of the traffic-free area as the experiment has proved so successful. It has attracted people to move back into the city centre, increased property and land values and enhanced the turnover of shops. Similarly, extensive pedestrianisation in **Munich**, supported by an excellent integrated transport system, has produced a spectacular rise in use and in trading profits.

This is one of those questions which needs vision, courage and staying power. In 1990, environmental artist Jim Lundy grassed over **Melbourne**'s Swanston Street in order to encourage the public to use it more. His action provoked a heated debate and led to the first pedestrianisation programme in central Melbourne. When the municipal administration of

Naples, elected in December 1993, decided to pedestrianise the seafront at weekends, it instantly became the city's most popular public promenade, animated with street performances, stalls and waterfront activities.

Other ideas include charging tolls to enter city centres, as in **Singapore**, where traffic was dramatically reduced, or the simple solution of restricting access to cars with even or uneven numbers as in **Milan** or **Athens** on days when pollution levels are particularly high. In **Florence** and other Italian cities access by car to the city centre is restricted to residents and permit holders.

- *Beating the weather*

'There is nothing you can do about the weather' is a common refrain often used to justify doing nothing. We have heard this so many times in Britain when people explain why it is impossible to open more pavement cafés or encourage street life. So how do they manage in colder cities such as **Oslo** or **Helsinki**? They put on an extra jumper, sit under a canopy and watch the world go by. It's amazing what can be done with a canopy.

In **Amsterdam**, Floris Guntenaar, an architect, has set up the Via Europa foundation, which specialises in building temporary structures to house performances and exhibitions in places at risk from unpredictable weather. These structures are designed to be quickly converted into indoor spaces should the weather become inclement.

Hot countries have also produced a crop of good examples. Visitors to the 1992 Expo in **Seville** were amazed by how cool it felt despite the huge crowds and scorching temperatures in the rest of the city. This was achieved by the extensive use of water jets, fountains, greenery and gazebos to create a more pleasant micro-climate on the site. More simply, shade and protection against the rain in the main square of **Valencia** was maximised by stretching a gigantic cloth from the roofs of buildings on one side of the square to those on the opposite side.

Once again it is the force of the simplicity of creativity that shines through, with the 'right' observation leading to an appropriate solution.

- *Genius loci*

Out of thousands of examples of creative ways of celebrating local identity and distinctiveness, those included here are but a small sample. In **Britain**, Common Ground has achieved a great deal through its campaign for local distinctiveness, including the development of parish maps, community orchards, community milestones and celebrations. Common Ground reminds us of what we often already know, but are in danger of forgetting. Their creativity lies in their ability to pinpoint the ancient details of our environment, which may be destroyed by rushing for big solutions.

Community arts projects in Britain, such as the Fishquay Festival in **North Shields**, which draws on the fishing heritage of the area to create a new civic ritual as well as an event that has helped regenerate the area, show how a local tradition can be reinvigorated.

In recent years many public art and environmental art commissions have attempted to re-establish – or create from scratch – a sense of place. During **Perth**'s 150th anniversary celebrations large paving stones were inserted in the main street, identifying each year with a particular individual relevant to the city's history. One example was Herb Elliot, the Olympic middle distance champion. At another extreme **Unna,** a medium sized town in the Ruhr, used local metal-working companies to make art objects under the guidance of experienced artists as part of its public art programme. Some of the artworks concerned themes related to the local steel industry. Since hundreds of local apprentices took part in making these, they do not attract graffiti and vandalism, as nearly every inhabitant has some link with the makers. By contrast, nearby **Bochum** has a sculpture by American artist Richard Serra, which local people feel was parachuted in, and which is constantly vandalised.

Italy is renowned for its 'feste' and 'sagre' events, invented by local people, generally with no public subsidy, simply to have a good time. They punctuate the civic calendar in ways that are relevant to each place. A small town on the foothills of a wooded mountain has a mushroom festival in the early autumn; a pig rearing area has a sausage festival, while grape growing and flower growing areas hold appropriate festivals at harvest time. Many of these initiatives are new. Visitors from Northern Europe are often amazed at the initiative and inventiveness of these small villages, yet if delicious mushrooms grow around you it's the obvious thing to celebrate.

In a housing estate in the Putuo district of **Shanghai** most local residents participate in singing and music competitions. Competing families perform from their balconies, while the audiences and judges assemble in the courtyard of the estate, which is transformed into a festival square with special lighting and food. Such events highlight the spirit of place of the estate as a whole, but also of individual households, which have the opportunity to express their personality through costumes, performance styles, choice of instruments and choreography.

The limit to all these expressions of creativity is that although they are wonderful for the duration, they do not transform the overall structure of daily life in the city – nor the way city governments operate. Politicians and policy-makers are rarely prepared to learn from the organisations which run events such as these.

- Young ideas

Children and teenagers are a source of fresh and often very clear ideas. Yet, as a report by the Junge Union of Bavaria recently claimed, children are the only citizens without political rights. Some cities have taken steps to change this. In 1991 **Unna** opened a children's office, where twice a week young people can discuss their ideas with the local authority. Politicians and officers are available, including the mayor, who can be consulted by the children once a month. Similarly the city of **Neuchâtel** in Switzerland set up a Youth Council for school-age children and a Youth Consultation Committee for representing 16 to 25 year olds.

While not going so far, other cities have made efforts to become more child friendly. **Birmingham** has opened a Centre for the Child with a focus on childcare, and **Edinburgh** started a 'child friendly' campaign in 1991, initially aimed at making pubs and shops more user friendly for children.

Many other cities are encouraging young people to express their ideas by setting up infrastructures for profitable cultural production. One example is **Sheffield** with its successful and expanding Cultural Industries Quarter, which comprises businesses and production facilities for popular music, film and video, including Red Tape, Britain's first municipal recording studios and rehearsal rooms. Local youth have access to special grants and equipment at much reduced prices.

In 1981 **Bologna** set up a holistic Youth Programme, cutting across departmental divisions, to address the inter-related social, cultural and economic needs of young people. It has encouraged self-managed forms of training which build on informal skills and attempt to bridge the gap between amateurism and professionalism. The municipality renovated its youth centres, encouraging young people to run them on their own or in co-operation with youth workers. The city council and the provincial council also supported youth enterprises, working both in traditional artisan crafts – leatherwork, precious metalwork, instrument-making – and in cultural industries similar to those developed in Sheffield. One of the Youth Programme's projects is 'Prophet in Your Own Country', under which the city council provides loans and grants to new talent and access to advice so that young people can set up businesses in the cultural sector. This is a way of ensuring that talent doesn't emigrate.[20]

The key idea in all these projects is to treat young people as a resource rather than as a problem.

Of course, old people can have young ideas too. In many cases, old age and retirement bring about a rediscovery of skills and abilities that have matured with experience. With time on their hands, and freedom from the pressures of work, many elderly people feel at last able to express themselves. The blossoming of the University of the Third Age in **Britain**, one of the fastest expanding informal education networks, is witness to this.

The European Year of Older People and Solidarity between Generations in 1993, initiated by the European Union, has contributed to highlighting awareness of the potential of older people. Again the category of older people is usually treated as a problem, or ignored altogether, rather than as a valuable resource. Given the ageing of urban populations in Western

Europe, it is surprising that elderly people are not consulted about urban policies which directly affect them. Nearly every product one uses could be reconceptualised in terms of the needs of the elderly. In 1993, the Royal College of Art held the Designing for Our Future Selves conference, which featured an interesting exhibition – 'Beyond the Zimmerframe' – showing how innovative ideas can help integrate older people into society and stimulate the new 50-plus market. The implicit ageism of those who plan for cities has meant that we know of no city that has a coherent strategy for improving the quality of life for its elderly population. Sadly the wisdom of the elderly remains underused.

- *Shifting time*

The opening page of **Milan**'s municipal five-year programme, published in 1990, stated that urban timetables had to be completely rethought with the needs of working women in mind, with major implications for shops and the provision of all types of services. They suggested staggered opening hours both to suit new lifestyle patterns and to have a positive effect on traffic volumes. Indeed, when did you last buy a pair of shoes at 9 o'clock in the morning?

Typically what happens in Britain is that most people working in city centres squeeze a bit of shopping and lunch into a half hour or an hour break. As city centre shops generally close at 5.30pm it is not surprising that the out-of-town shopping centres, which are open until 7 or 8pm are packed, thereby decreasing the vitality of the city itself. There are numerous, isolated attempts to keep some stores open later – especially initiatives on late-night Thursday shopping – but this is rarely part of a comprehensive programme involving public transport (which winds down dramatically after 6pm), entertainment, marketing and policing. Attempts have been made to bridge the 5.30 to 7.30pm dead period through variations on the idea of a Happy Hour. In **Leeds,** for example, the city council used its week-long St Valentine's Fair in February to create a carnival atmosphere in the city's town hall square with fairground cafés, restaurants and bars. In the words of Jon Trickett, leader of Leeds City Council:

"After an initial amount of pump priming it costs the council tax payer not a penny. Such events can encourage big retailers to experiment with extending their hours to 7 or 8 in the evening so that the awful gap between the offices closing and the theatres and restaurants filling, when many cities die, can be filled. Councils must not stop providing services at 5.30pm. The streets must be cleaned for the evening as well as the day. Public toilets must not be locked up and buses and trains become infrequent."[21]

In **Newcastle** they have used the Happy Hour more comprehensively for the same purpose. On various days of the week, some bars and restaurants reduce their prices substantially in order to encourage people to stay in the city centre and use its facilities. The prices are so low that it is hardly worth going home and cooking your own food.

In **Manchester**, in September 1993, opening hours for licensed premises were extended to midnight for pubs and bars, and to 4am for clubs. More people used the city centre as a result. Compared with the previous month, alcohol-related incidents and total arrests in the city centre decreased by 14 per cent and 43 per cent respectively. Taxi companies reported 'increased trade and less aggravation', and the police were 'pleasantly surprised' by the effect of the initiative on public order.[22]

The creative use of time is largely unexplored. In the context of sustainability, imaginative urban timetabling could save resources and improve quality of life. Traffic congestion could be reduced by staggering office hours; services of all kinds could be made more available to people from the regional catchment area; life in the city could become less hectic by spreading activity through a larger amount of time. In Nordic cities proposals are being considered to shift winter working, with a later start to the working day, to ensure people have extra daylight for leisure uses. Being creative is also about being able to grasp the potential of invisible resources such as time.

- Greening the city

There are an increasing number of greening initiatives in cities all over the world, concerned with cycling and recycling, pollution control, energy saving, environmental auditing, bringing nature into the city and raising awareness. But few administrations have fully explored the concept of greening.

The British Environment City movement is one example of how efforts can be made to implement an environmental perspective that infuses every aspect of city life. **Leicester** became Britain's first Environment City in 1990. Environ, the organisation running the project, has a set of think-tanks drawing from the public, private, community and academic sectors. They consider issues such as the built, natural and social environment; the economy and work; energy; transport; waste and pollution. Among its dozens of projects, Environment City has carried out environmental reviews and given landscape advice for local companies and public sector clients; provided greening grants to industry; set up an environment friendly showhouse – Ecohouse – and organised an annual energy week; assisted in cutting energy consumption in municipal buildings; helped install low energy street lights and undertaken a survey of 4,000 private gardens to assess their importance to city wildlife; and raised money through Leicester's Asian community to reafforest a holy Hindu site in India. They are now building a 24-mile round-city cycle and pedestrian route; municipal purchasing policies have been adjusted to take account of their environmental friendliness; and 'green accounts' have been made with 200 charities to help in the collection of recyclable waste throughout the city. **Middlesbrough** is also part of the Environment City movement, and has undertaken similar initiatives.

One of the outcomes of the Earth Summit in Rio in June 1992 was Local Agenda 21, a programme setting urban sustainability targets for the 21st century which will affect the work of every local authority in Britain. Given that the concept of sustainability is holistic, and requires lateral thinking and corporate working for it to be effective, Local Agenda 21 should encourage a totally new way of looking at urban development.

- Making something out of nothing

Sometimes the work of individuals can produce successful innovations in the most unlikely places. About 20 years ago, **Hay-on-Wye** on the Welsh borders was a small agricultural backwater. Yet the single-minded initiative of Richard Booth has led to Hay becoming a Book City with 42 bookshops, now the major economic sector in the town. Other large booksellers, who later moved in, organised a literary festival of national importance, which has helped develop the town's appeal to tourists. Booth has now developed a European network of Book Cities, with counterparts in Belgium and France.

In the Tiber valley in Tuscany, the town of **Pieve S. Stefano** celebrates the annual Festival of Diaries with prizes for the best diaries, thus facilitating their publication. The town has established a National Diary Archive and is marketing itself as Diary City.

The mountain town of **Apricale** in Liguria in northern Italy had been declining as population moved to larger urban centres in search of work. As a partial response, the remaining local inhabitants and some invited artists were encouraged to paint murals depicting scenes from local life throughout the town. In this way, the previously unknown town became part of the tourist route. New restaurants opened and the town began to revive.

Copredy, a large village near Banbury, has used the annual Fairport Convention reunion to regenerate its local economy. The small local shop has over the years become a supermarket and voluntary organisations within the village derive most of their annual income from the support services they provide for the event.

Much can also be made out of things generally regarded as unsightly, such as car parks and sewers. The Opera House car park in **Cologne**, for example, includes shops selling car maintenance products. **Launceston** in Tasmania is proud of its new network of sewers and now organises popular sewer tours, while a tourist operator in **Sydney** even offers tours of 'ugly Sydney'.

What these examples show is that with humour and panache you can turn anything to your benefit. The creativity here is the capacity to look at things in an upside down way.

- Weakness into strength

Much has been written about **Glasgow** and its long-term regeneration strategy. A minor, but interesting, example is the way it turned a perceived weakness into a strength. In assessing its assets, the Greater Glasgow Tourist Board concluded that the weather was a major problem. Then they had a brainwave. Since the weather is even worse in Iceland, the board decided to market Glasgow to Icelanders as a kind of

Riviera. The strategy has paid off and Glasgow today is firmly on the map for Icelandic tour operators.

In 1956 the Washington Gas Company abandoned its site facing downtown **Seattle** across Lake Union. The council acquired it and in 1970 commissioned landscape architect Richard Haag to convert it into a park. Haag became fascinated by the generator towers and intricate pipework of the old gas plant. He proposed that large elements of the works be retained as the core of a new kind of urban park. In the face of relentless opposition from the local press and large sections of the public, the Gas Works Park was opened in 1975. It features an old exhauster building converted into a children's play barn, and a re-roofed boiler house transformed into a picnic shelter; contaminated soil has been grassed over and a great mound has been made out of waste, topped by a monumental sundial, from which there are spectacular views of lake and city. As Michael Middleton comments in his description of the park:

"So much of industry's detritus is regarded unthinkingly… as ugly and depressing… Gas Works Park is very much a fun place… and the level of use has outstripped all expectations. The park is easy now to take for granted, but how many towns one wonders would have had the courage and imagination to do likewise? 'I'm amazed,' says Haag, 'every time I go down there that I actually pulled it off.'" [23]

Seattle city council has never been frightened by bold ideas. It has organised World's Fairs, created freeway parks and implemented a visually striking programme of artworks in public places.

Cities falling on hard times have the problem of declining property values. Forests of 'to let' and 'for sale' signs in city centres can have the effect of accelerating the spiral of decline by discouraging potential investors. However, low rents and property prices also offer the opportunity to start a process of regeneration. All over the world, local authorities or private entrepreneurs have offered cheap accommodation to artists, artisans and small businesses in workshops, managed workspaces and incubator units – often in redundant industrial areas close to city centres. Examples range from the Jewellery Quarter and the Custard Factory in **Birmingham**, the Noisel Centre d'Art et de Culture in **Marne la Vallée** in France, the Brickbottom Artists Co-operative in **Boston** and the Cable Factory in **Helsinki.** Developments of this kind in Europe now have their own network, known as Trans Europe Halles, with offices in Paris.

One small example is **Huddersfield**, which has become Britain's poetry capital. Low rents and the cheaper cost of living attracted a number of poets, who through their own contacts and support from Kirklees Metropolitan Council created a snowball effect so that poetry events of national significance are held regularly. Related national organisations have moved there and, for those specialising in this activity, Huddersfield's image has changed.

The presence of artists and other cultural producers in declining urban areas helps restore vitality, develop a positive image, create additional employment and break cycles of decline. However, the risk is that in the medium term areas that artists have made fashionable may increase in value so much that they themselves are pushed out.

What these tales demonstrate is that a weakness can become a strength if looked at from an oblique angle. A city may have a bad image in the eyes of some, but contain exactly what others are looking for.

- Creating momentum through catalysts

Participatory workshops, conferences, symposia, experiments and pilot projects, festivals and prestigious sports and cultural events that attract media coverage can facilitate imaginative scenario building and visioning. The American idea of holding Urban Design Action Team (UDAT) workshops is one means of bringing together people with different backgrounds, interests and perspectives to discuss the future of an urban area. They can be no-holds-barred events where ideas spring up and connections are made that would not happen within formal structures. This creative process often leads to bolder visions which are sometimes able to overcome problems previously seen as insoluble.

In 1991, the London Borough of **Haringey** initiated a UDAT to rethink the uses of the Wood Green district and the Alexandra Palace complex. UDAT-type processes have been used successfully by community groups in developing viable alternatives to developers' plans, as in **King's Cross** in London.

The 'Estate Romana', a programme of primarily night-time cultural events in **Rome**, organised by the left-controlled city council from 1977 to 1985, involved the closure of city centre streets to traffic as well as the use of strategic floodlighting. Major archaeological sites – the Coliseum, the Appian Way and the Circus Maximus – were used for large, popular cultural events. This stimulated a lively public debate about the uses of the city both during the day and at night. Bold proposals emerged, such as one to dig up Via dei Fori Imperiali, a major central thoroughfare, in order to create the city's largest archaeological park and a much needed green oasis. Before this proposal could be implemented, however, the administration lost power.

In 1974, **Galveston**, Texas, set up a Dickens Festival to highlight the decaying – indeed Dickensian – state of the waterfront area, which had been built in the 19th century. As a consequence a historic preservation trust was set up that has gradually regenerated the area.

In the deprived peripheral housing estate of **Easterhouse** in Glasgow local residents formed a festival society in 1980. It successfully initiated a series of arts projects, including the construction of Europe's largest mosaic mural. These activities were instrumental in raising people's confidence and creating an organisational focus on which wider regeneration initiatives could be based. The process generated the Greater Easterhouse Partnership, to co-ordinate public, private and voluntary sector work, such as training and economic development projects, for the enhancement of the area.

- Branding

Branding is a way of identifying a place with particular attributes. The minute you arrive in **Montpellier**, for example, you are told what the city is and what it wants to become: it has been made into a narrative. If you arrive by car, you are greeted by a welcome in a dozen languages, including Japanese – this symbolises the city's cosmopolitanism and international orientation. Entering the city, you notice that the streets are all named after scientists such as Albert Einstein or Alfred Nobel –this is the innovative enterprises zone of the city. The message is that Montpellier is future-oriented. As you walk around there are all kinds of ecological messages about the city and its newly built cycleways – this signals its environmental friendliness. When you finally reach the main square there is a mobile health screening unit – a statement that Montpellier wants its citizens to be healthy. So before you have had your first coffee, you have been told a story about Montpellier.

The creative innovation here is thinking through the process of getting into the city and reading it like a book.

Ironbridge near Telford is also a good example of branding. Now known throughout the world, it is home to the world's first iron bridge. Interesting, but not particularly remarkable. However, as the area was one of the cradles of the industrial revolution, it contains within a 10-mile radius a large number of smaller attractions – potteries, mineshafts and other old industrial buildings. By marketing this collection of smaller attractions under the overarching concept of 'Ironbridge' critical mass has been created. It thus has much more impact on visitors and investors. The lesson here is that 'more can be made out of less' by taking a wider territorial view, one which goes beyond your immediate locality.

- Using technology to make connections

In **Karlsruhe** the city council and the state government of Baden-Württemberg re-established the link between science and art by developing a Centre for Arts and Media Technology, linked with a College of Design. It seeks to harness the potential of new developments such as computer music, computer animation and computer-based performing arts in order to produce more broadly based commercial applications, which they hope will strengthen the city's economic base. The board of the centre includes physicists, engineers, information scientists, politicians and artists.

Grenoble was one of the first European cities to systematically supply individual households with information held by the local authority through the Minitel network. Residents were able to access municipal library stocks; vote on local referenda; find out about environmental health, leisure, rubbish collection and other council services; and even be informed about the agendas and outcomes of council meetings.

By enabling households to receive amounts of information which until recently would have been unthinkable, fibre optic cabling will multiply opportunities for cities to be creative. For example, it will be possible for private or public sector or joint operators to provide services such as video on demand and interactive TV. Some cities, like **Biarritz** and **Montpellier** in southern France are already well advanced on this road, although, because of production costs, they have found it difficult to make local programmes.

The key point about these examples is their use of technologies as a way of creating synergies and multiplying opportunities, which may produce results that cannot be predicted at the outset.

- *Beyond the public/private divide*

In a world where the division between the public and the private sector has been cemented for so long, forming a well working public/private partnership is itself a creative act. The British government's City Challenge programme has given a big boost to this process, because forming a partnership between the public, private and voluntary sectors was the condition for obtaining a grant. But many of these partnerships underachieve. One of the reasons is the relative weakness of private sector actors in most British cities. In the USA, where private sector partners substantially contribute to partnerships – in terms of both finance and commitment – these initiatives tend to be more successful.

Town centre management is a spatially focused and practical way of getting together different interest groups within a city to solve problems. One of the best models is that of **High Wycombe**. This consists of a Town Centre Association, which has monthly meetings with the business community; a town centre forum – a consultative body – meeting quarterly and comprising representatives of amenity groups, youth, disabled people, pensioners, the police, the highway authority, Wycombe District Council and the Town Centre Association; and Wycombe District Council's Town Centre Action Team, with six multi-disciplinary officers with experience that ranges from marketing to engineering, who report to the council's main policy committee, and produce an annual report to monitor outputs, as well as regular town centre newsletters to disseminate information.[24]

About 75 towns in Britain have appointed town centre managers with janitorial, managerial and promotional roles. Unfortunately most town centre managers have a background in security, retailing or marketing, and in many cases are not equipped to view the town centre holistically. They often do not understand the city's history and of its cultures and subcultures. They also tend to focus primarily on the daytime retailing needs of the town centre, often to the exclusion of the night-time economy and of other aspects of economic, social and cultural life.

Although **Bristol** has over the last 10 years become more important as a regional media centre, its local authority felt that the city's profile was weak. Historically the city had been fortunate in having some local developers who pushed forward two key waterfront projects – the Arnolfini and Watershed – as part of a planning gain agreement with the city council. These landmark developments, market forces and the perceived quality of life of the area subsequently made the city attractive to photographers, artists and independent film-makers. Nevertheless, the city council had not played any leading role in encouraging policy initiatives or strategy development until 1992, when it helped set up the Bristol Cultural Development Partnership (BCDP). This public/private partnership aims to drive cultural policy-making in the city. The Chamber of

Commerce is the leading private sector organisation, funding the partnership to the tune of 50 per cent through contributions from individual members. The partnership has ensured that the city keeps abreast of key initiatives and potential resources for cultural urban regeneration. It has sought to attract film festivals and other cultural events to Bristol and has sought funding for a new performing arts centre. As a mixed public and private organisation, it has been able to harness resources which up till now the city council working on its own had simply been unable to mobilise. BCDP is a creative idea – the first independent agency formulating and implementing the strategic cultural policies of a large European city.

In 1985, the city state of **Hamburg**, the local chamber of commerce and the city's 10 most important banks set up the Hamburg Business Development Corporation, with the remit of attracting new firms to the city and supporting existing ones. In its first five years of existence, the Corporation attracted 387 firms and created 16,000 new jobs.

In **Rennes**, the mayor established Codespar, a consortium bringing together business, the unions and local authorities in the region in order to prepare strategic plans for the area. Codespar identified electronics and communication, health and the bio-industries as the key sectors for the growth of the local economy. Codespar successfully set up the Rennes-Atalante science park, where Canon has recently located its European research centre, and which has become a showcase for the city's economic development strategy.[25]

A creative partnership allows the different partners to play to their respective strengths. The private sector is usually good at getting things done in the most efficient way, particularly in competitive situations. The voluntary sector is good at articulating local views as well as communicating with users and developing a sense of ownership. The key strength of the public sector, on the other hand, is maintaining a strategic overview and ensuring that the broader public objectives of the partnership are achieved.

- Developing self-reliance and countering prejudice

Exercising the muscle of self-reliance is one of the best ways of building up self-confidence and therefore encouraging people to be more creative. Two simple ideas in two cities with very serious homelessness problems have had a small but symbolically significant effect on how the homeless see themselves and are seen by other people.

In **New York**, homeless people collect empty tin cans because for each can the collector receives money from the city administration, while in **London** *The Big Issue* weekly magazine is sold by homeless people who receive half the sale price. While both initiatives are clearly not substitutes for proper jobs or accommodation, they at least give participants some self-respect and confidence. According to the letters page of *The Big Issue*, selling the paper has for many been an impulse to make a fresh start.

- Giving people a say

A creative city needs constant feedback from its citizens. The act of voting every four or five years is insufficient to convey people's ideas to local government.

Consultation procedures are well developed in many cities. They take place through consultative committees, as in **Neuchâtel**; neighbourhood and community councils, as in

Middlesbrough; citizens' offices, as in **Unna**; and communication plans for local authority projects, as in **Bradford**. While such bodies often exert pressure and are usually taken seriously, their deliberations are not binding for the local authority.

Some cities have gone beyond consultation by developing ideas to extend and sharpen local democracy. The city of **Québec** in Canada, capital of the state with the same name, has developed an effective system of citizen participation. In two urban districts local people elect citizen bodies with direct rights of initiating proposals and making decisions which are binding on the local authority.[26]

Other interesting ideas emerging in American cities include those establishing voter juries, vetoes and feedback. Juries assess the pros and cons of contested policy proposals; vetoes give citizens the right to call consultative referenda on controversial council decisions; feedback experiments engage people in deliberation on local issues through combined TV and telephone networks built by cable authorities. One example is the 'Conversation with **Oregon**' televised meeting held by the Democrat governor Barbara Roberts, to which a random cross-section of 80,000 Oregon citizens was invited. A second example is the televote organised by the State of **Hawaii** to elicit input from the general public during a state-wide constitutional convention – an event which traditionally lacked any public involvement. A representative sample of voters were mailed an info pack. A call-back time was arranged when the researchers phoned voters for their responses, which were generally responsible and sophisticated.[27]

- Checking out progress

As yet, no large city has a comprehensive system for assessing where it is now, deciding where it wants to go and monitoring its progress in getting there. But many cities have developed sophisticated information systems and statistical offices. The municipal information office of **Helsinki** is a particularly good example. However, the most impressive initiative for its strategic orientation is the experiment called 'Oregon Benchmarks: Setting Measurable Standards for Progress'. Put in place by the state of **Oregon** to track progress in achieving objectives in fields as diverse as teenage pregnancy, air quality, personal income, infant mortality, Aids cases, crime, attendances at arts events and business start up rates, the information generated forces decision-makers to be more accountable for success or failure.

This is a simple idea, which until recently was dismissed as either too impractical or too risky by city administrations.

Conclusions

What is striking is that so many ideas used by cities appear simple and even obvious in retrospect. They point to the importance of clarity of observation based on essentials, and appropriateness to purpose. They seem to grasp the totality of the problem in one. This is what gives them the 'eureka' effect. Everything is seen as a resource, including things commonly regarded as liabilities. The courage of sticking to your plans in the face of hostility and adversity seems paramount. There is often a need to go against the grain of supposed common sense, conventional wisdom and narrow commercial imperatives.

The key requirements for success include the following:

New ways of talking - different people must talk to each other in different ways, breaking down the normal debating routes and networks to allow a more open system which forces those with different skills and disciplines to talk and listen to each other.

New ways of mapping - new forms of local research and monitoring are needed to define local aspirations, desires, actual and potential problems and trends.

New ways of describing things - descriptions of problems, solutions and ambitions may make more sense if the old vocabulary is cleared away and less jargon used. The language of traditional geography is often inadequate to identify resources such as atmosphere, the quality of public and social life, cultural vibrancy and other characteristics of the 'soft infrastructure' of places.

New forms of research and development - Private sector businesses would die very quickly without an active research and development budget. City governments should encourage experimental and pilot projects. Failure should be tolerated, and analysed in a critical but constructive way.

New selection processes - These must be put in place to select, exploit and evaluate ideas. Making these ideas public at some stage is vital. This could happen in the same way as ideas and projects for new buildings and public spaces are made public through exhibitions following architectural and design competitions.

Removal of obstacles - The various structures and bureaucracies which prevent or discourage creative thinking should be dismantled or at least neutralised.

Orchestration - The tempo and style of pulling ideas and actions together is not that of a perfectly rehearsed symphony, but more like that of a jazz jam session. Innovation and improvisation are all-important to the creative result.

Sense of direction - There must be a strategy which provides impetus and encouragement, but leaves the city space to develop naturally as well.

Monitoring - Different forms of monitoring must be put in place to check on progress and enable cities to share and learn from their experiences. Situations may differ, but there is no reason for cities to have to reinvent the wheel.

Endnotes

1 Harvey, D. (1990) *The Condition of Postmodernity.* Oxford: Blackwell, p102

2 Geddes, P. (1907) *Cities: Being an Introduction to the Study of Civics*, London: University of London Extension Lecture Syllabus

3 Mumford, L. (1961) *The City in History*, London: Secker and Warburg

4 Jacobs, J. (1979) *The Death and Life of Great American Cities*, London: Pelican

5 Anderson, A. (1994) 'Cities within cities', New Scientist, The future supplement, 15 October, p15

6 Evans, B. (1994) 'Planning, sustainability and the chimera of community', *Town and Country Planning,* April, pp106-7

7 Sharpe, W. and Wallock, L. (1987) *Visions of the Modern City*, London: Johns Hopkins University Press

8 Melvin Webber quoted in Sharpe and Wallock, *op. cit.*, chapter 1

9 Williams, R. (1983) *Keywords*, Glasgow: Fontana, p84

10 De Bono, E. (1993) *Serious Creativity*, London: HarperCollins, p42

11 Quoted in Barry, A. (1993), 'The impact of ideas', *Intercity*, December-January

12 Melucci, A. *et al.* (1994) *Creatività miti, discorsi, processi,* Milan: Feltrinelli, pp235-42

13 Melucci, *op. cit.*, p231

14 Girouard, M. (1990) *The English Town*, New Haven, Conn.: Yale University Press

15 See, on this point, De Bono *op. cit.*, p109

16 Burke, P. (1974) *Venice and Amsterdam: A Study of Seventeenth Century Elites*, London: Temple Smith

17 See Brown, B. and Perkins, D. (1992) 'Disruption in place attachment' in Altman, I. and Low, S. (eds) *Place Attachment*, New York: Plenum Press, and Eyles, G. (1989) 'The geography of everyday life' in Gregor, D. and Walford, R. (eds) *Horizons in Human Geography*, London: Macmillan

18 Young, K. (1994) *Quality of Life in Cities - An Overview and Guide to the Literature*, London: London Research Centre

19 Khan, N. and Worpole, K. (1992) *Travelling Hopefully: A Study of the Arts in the Transport System*, London: Comedia & the Gulbenkian Foundation

20 Bloomfield, J. (1993) 'Bologna: a laboratory for cultural enterprise' in Bianchini, F. and Parkinson, M. (eds) *Cultural Policy and Urban Regeneration: the West European Experience*, Manchester: Manchester University Press

21 Trickett, J. (1994) 'The 24 hour city: retailing as animation', *Regenerating Cities*, 6, pp10-11

22 Lovatt, A. (1994) *More Hours in The Day*, Manchester: Manchester Institute for Popular Culture, Manchester Metropolitan University

23 Middleton, M (1987) *Man Made the Town*, London: Bodley Head

24 URBED (1994) *Vital and Viable Town Centres: Meeting the Challenge*, London: HMSO, p77

25 Parkinson,M.et al. (1992) *Urbanization and the Function of Cities in the European Community*, Brussels: Commission of the European Communities

26 Bertlesman Foundation (1993) *Carl Bertlelsmann Prize: Democracy and Efficiency in Local Government*, Gutersloh: Bertlesmann Foundation

27 Bartle, M. (1994) 'Initiatives and experiments', *Demos Quarterly, 3*

Further Reading

Adonis, A. and Mulgan, G. (1994) 'Back to Greece: the scope for direct democracy', *Demos Quarterly*, 3.

Andersson, A. E. (1987) *Culture, creativity and economic development in a regional context*, Strasbourg: Council of Europe.

Arieti, S. (1979) *Creatività: la sintesi magica*, Rome: Astrolabio.

Austin, J. H. (1978) *Chase, Chance and Creativity: The Lucky Art of Novelty*, New York: Columbia University Press.

Barron, F. (1969) *Creative Person and Creative Process*, New York: Holt, Rinehart and Winston.

Becker, M. B. (1981) *Medieval Italy: Contrasts and Creativity*, Bloomington, Ind.: University of Indiana Press.

Becker, T. (1994) 'Electrifying democracy', *Demos Quarterly*, 3.

Bianchini, F. (1991) 'Urban cultural policy', *National Arts and Media Strategy Discussion Documents*, 40, London: Arts Council.

Bianchini and Parkinson, M. (eds) (1993) *Cultural Policy and Urban Regeneration: The West European Experience*, Manchester: Manchester University Press.

Boden, M. A. (1990) *The Creative Mind: Myths and Mechanisms*, London: Weidenfeld and Nicolson.

Buttimer, A. (ed) (1983) *Creativity and Context*, Lund, CWK Gleerup.

Cable, V. (1994) *The World's New Fissures: Identities in Crisis*, London: Demos.

De Bono, E. (1993) *Serious Creativity*, London: Harper Collins.

Dervin, D. (1990) *Creativity and Culture: A Psychoanalytic Study of the Creative Process in the Arts, Science and Culture*, London: Associated University Press.

Drucker, P. (1985) *Innovation and Entrepreneurship*, New York: Harper.

Ennals, K. and O'Brien, J. (1990) *The Enabling Role of Local Authorities*, London, Public Finance Foundation.

Gardner, H. (1982) *Art, Mind and Brain: A Cognitive Approach to Creativity*, New York: Basic Books.

Gardner, H. (1988) 'Creativity: an interdisciplinary perspective', *Creativity Research Journal*, 1.

Gardner, H. (1991) *The Unschooled Mind*, London: Fontana.

Gardner, H. (1993) *Creative Minds*, New York: Basic Books

Garroni, E. (1978) 'Creatività', in *Enciclopedia Einaudi*, vol. 4, Turin: Einaudi.

Guilford, J. P. (1950) 'Creativity', *American Psychologist*, 1.

Handy, C. (1994) *The Future of Work*, London: Hutchinson

Harvey, D. (1990) *The Condition of Postmodernity*, Oxford: Blackwell.

Healey, P. (1989) 'Planning for the 1990s', *Department of Town and Country Planning Working Papers Series*, 7, Newcastle upon Tyne: University of Newcastle upon Tyne.

Henry, J. (1990) *Creative Management*, London: Sage/Open University Press.

Jaoui, H. (1975) *La Créativité*, Paris: Seghers.

Koenehsberger, D. (1979) *Renaissance Man and Creative Thinking*, Hassocks: Harvester.

Leadbeater, C. and Mulgan, G. (1994) 'Lean democracy and the leadership vacuum', *Demos Quarterly*, 3.

Lee, V. (1976) *Intelligence and Creativity*, Milton Keynes: Open University Press.

Machlup, F. (1984) *Knowledge: Its Creation, Distribution and Economic Significance*, Princeton: Princeton University Press.

Melucci, A. *et al*. (1994) *Creatività: miti, discorsi, processi*, Milan: Feltrinelli.

Morgan, G. (1993) *Imaginization: The Art of Creative Management*, Newbury Park: Sage.

Nystrom, H. (1979) *Creativity and Innovation*, Chichester: Wiley.

Osborn, D. and Gaebler, T. (1992) *Reinventing Government*, Reading MA: Addison Wesley.

Ohmae, K. (1982) *The Mind of the Strategist*, New York: McGraw-Hill.

Ray, M. and Myers, R. (1986) *Creativity in Business*, New York: Doubleday.

Robinson, G. and Rundell J. (eds) (1993) *Rethinking Imagination: Culture and Creativity*, London: Routledge.

Rothenberg, A. (1980) *The Creative Process in Art, Science and Other Fields*, Chicago: University of Chicago Press.

Runco, M. A. and Albert R. S. (eds) (1990) *Theories of Creativity*, Newbury Park: Sage.

Sharpe, W. and Wallock, L. (1987) *Visions of the Modern City*, London: Johns Hopkins University Press.

Sennett, R. (1970) *The Uses of Disorder*, New York: Knopf.

Sternberg, R. J. (1988) *The Nature of Creativity: Contemporary Psychological Perspectives*, New York: Cambridge University Press.

Storr, A. (1972) *The Dynamics of Creation*, London: Secker and Warburg.

Sveiby, K. E. and Lloyd, T. (1987) *Managing Knowhow*, London: Bloomsbury.

Taylor, C. W. (ed) (1972) *Climate for Creativity*, New York: Pergamon.

Taylor, I. A. and Getzels, J. W. (eds) (1975) *Perspectives in Creativity*, Chicago: Aldine.

Weisberg, R. W. (1993) *Creativity: Beyond the Myth of Genius*, New York: W. H. Freeman.

The following papers, all published by Comedia in 1994 in The Creative City Working Papers series are available at £10 each (except for 'Artists and the creative city', which is £6) from Comedia, The Round, Bournes Green, Near Stroud, Gloucestershire GL6 7NL. Tel: 01452 770624. Fax: 01452 770596.

Bianchini, F. and Landry, C. 'Indicators of a creative city: a methodology for assessing urban vitality and viability', ISBN 1 873667 90 6.

Ebert, R., Gnad, F. and Kunzmann, K. 'The creative city: concepts and preconditions', ISBN 1 873667 85 X.

Ghilardi Santacatterina, L. 'Artists and the creative city', ISBN 1 873667 06 X.

Other Demos publications available for £5.95 post free from Demos, 9 Bridewell Place, London EC4V 6AP.

Reconnecting Taxation by Geoff Mulgan, Director of Demos, and Robin Murray, adviser to the Government of Ontario.
ISBN 1 898309 00 0

An End to Illusions by Alan Duncan, Conservative MP for Rutland and Melton. ISBN 1 898309 05 1

Transforming the Dinosaurs by Sir Douglas Hague, Associate Fellow of Templeton College, Oxford. ISBN 1 898309 10 8

The Parenting Deficit by Amitai Etzioni, Professor of Sociology at George Washington University. ISBN 1 898309 20 5

Sharper Vision by Ian Hargreaves, Editor of the Independent. ISBN 1 898309 25 6

The World's New Fissures by Vincent Cable, Director of the International Economics Programme at the Royal Institute for International Affairs. ISBN 1 898309 35 3

The Audit Explosion by Michael Power, lecturer in Accounting and Finance and Coopers & Lybrand Fellow at the London School of Economics and Political Science. ISBN 1 898 309 30 2

The Mosaic of Learning: Schools and Teachers for the Next Century by David Hargreaves, Professor of Education at Cambridge University. ISBN 1 898 309 45 0

Alone Again: Ethics after Certainty by Zygmunt Bauman, Emeritus Professor of Sociology at Leeds University. ISBN 1 898 309 40 X

No Turning Back: Generations and the Genderquake by Helen Wilkinson, who is currently on sabbatical from the BBC. ISBN 1 898 309 75 2

The Common Sense of Community by Dick Atkinson, founder of the Phoenix Centre, Birmingham. ISBN 1 898309 80 9.

The Demos Quarterly

Issue 1 featured Howard Gardner on *'Opening Minds'* and a series of articles on education. Other contributors included John Stewart and Amitai Etzioni.

Issue 2 is titled *'The End of Unemployment: Bringing Work to Life'*. Contributors included Rosabeth Moss Kanter, Paul Ormerod, Martin Wolf and Douglas Hague.

Issue 3, *'Lean Democracy'*. Featured articles by Geoff Mulgan and Charles Leadbeater on *'lean democracy'* and a collection of articles on juries, electronic democracy and other future forms of democracy.

Issue 4, *'Liberation Technology'*. contains a collection of articles on the development of communications technology.

Demos is a registered charity. It is financed by voluntary donations from individuals, foundations and companies. The views expressed in publications are those of the authors alone. They do not represent Demos' institutional viewpoint.